Rock Lead
TECHNIQUES

by Nick Nolan and Danny Gill

T0055381

To access audio visit:
www.halleonard.com/mylibrary

Enter Code
5579-7421-2268-7629

ISBN 978-0-7935-7380-6

7777 W. BLUEMOUND RD. P.O. BOX 13819 MILWAUKEE, WI 53213

Visit Hal Leonard Online at
www.halleonard.com

CONTENTS

	Page	Audio Track
About the Authors	4	
Credits	4	
Tuning Notes	4	1
Chapter 1: Picking Technique	5	2–30
Chapter 2: Three-Note-Per-String Scales	11	
Chapter 3: Picking Licks	13	
Sequences	13	31–45
Licks	17	46–50
String Skipping	18	51–55
Fingerpicking	20	56–66
Chapter 4: Sweep Picking	22	67–78
Chapter 5: Harmonics	28	
Natural Harmonics	28	79–82
Fretted Harmonics	31	
Tap Harmonics	31	83–85
Harp Harmonics	32	86–88
Pinch Harmonics	33	89–90
Chapter 6: Solo Construction	35	91–95
Guitar Notation Legend	39	

ABOUT THE AUTHORS

Danny Gill left and Nick Nolan right.

Nick Nolan comes from Port Huron, Michigan where he began his professional playing career at the age of sixteen. He then went to G.I.T. on the Eddie Van Halen Scholarship and graduated with honors. After graduating, Nick became an instructor at G.I.T., teaching and writing curriculum for such subjects as: Rock Lead Guitar, Rock Rhythm Guitar, and the Rhythm Section Workshop, as well as teaching Music Reading, Harmony and Theory, Ear Training, and Modern Rock Performance.

Nick is also an active session player in Los Angeles, playing guitar on such T.V. series as: "Melrose Place," "Star Search" (as house guitarist), and "High Tide." You may have also heard Nick on the cartoons: "Bill and Ted's Excellent Adventure," "Back to the Future" (CBS), "Where's Waldo?" (CBS), "Super Mario Brothers" (NBC), "Captain Planet" (FOX), "Exosquad" (Universal), "What a Mess" (DIC), "Don Coyote" (Hanna-Barbera), "Mr. Magoo" (Disney), and "The Funtastic World of Hanna-Barbera."

Nick has also just released his first CD, titled *Up & Down & Back Again* on Standing 8 Records (P.O. Box 5280, North Hollywood, CA 91616)

Danny Gill recorded his first record in 1990 with Hericane Alice (Atlantic Records). Since then, he has gone on to record and tour with Arcade, Medicine Wheel, and will debut his new band (still looking for a name at press time) in 1998 on MCA records. His songs have appeared on numerous network T.V. shows and major motion picture soundtracks. Danny has also released a Star Licks video entitled *Modern Rock Guitar*. He currently teaches at Musicians Institute in Hollywood, California where his classes include Rock Rhythm Guitar, Rock Lead Guitar, and Single String Technique.

CREDITS

Nick Nolan: guitar
Danny Gill: guitar
Ian Mayo: bass
Tim Pedersen: drums

Recorded at M.I. Studios by Howard Karp
Photos: Kathrin Kraft

Nick thanks:
My wife Hiko (for everything), and Rob and Mick at Hoshino (for the great Talman)

Danny thanks:
My wife Alexandra for being my wife Alexandra and all of my family for everything else.

Editor's notes:

Follow the audio icons (◆) in the book. Use track 1 to help you tune.

A short "introduction" or "tag" may precede or follow the main lick of each figure, to give it a better sense of context. However, only the main lick itself appears transcribed in each case.

CHAPTER 1
PICKING TECHNIQUE

A subject that comes up a lot at G.I.T. is *picking technique*. There is no one "best" way to pick—but there are some bad ways (in terms of speed and clarity). You'll know if you've got some bad habits if you've been practicing a lot and still can't get any faster—or, if you're playing as fast as you want but it's always sloppy.

After years of practicing and teaching, we've come up with a method that will help get your picking fast and clean and works in any style. This method is naturally arrived at by many guitarists. In fact, we've had the opportunity to talk to some of the best technical players around when developing this picking style.

One last word before we start: Getting your picking together takes determination, patience, and practice. No one just picks up a guitar and starts blazing. You'll need to set time aside daily to become a good picker. The amount of time is up to you. Some of you may be looking to just pick up a little speed and clarity. Others may want to become real shredders.

Hand placement

How you hold your pick, how you position your hand, and how you attack the note all add up to how efficient your picking technique is. The key to speed and accuracy is *relaxation.* Try this: Hold your pick between your thumb and first finger (see Picture 1).

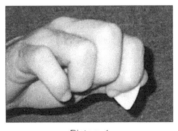

Picture 1

Picture 2

Now, plop your hand down on the guitar so the edge of your hand just touches the bridge saddles (see Picture 2). This is how your hand should look when picking. Compare this to how you normally pick and make note of the differences.

Attacking a note

There are many ways to attack a string. Some of you may tense up your forearm and shake your hand up and down—others may wiggle your fingers. We're going to talk about using your wrist to attack the note. Think of your hand as just a big "pick holder"; it doesn't make any adjustments during picking. Make sure your forearm is relaxed. The only motion is from your wrist. It is similar to turning a key inside a lock—a twisting motion.

Look at the series of pictures below and try to copy them:

Ready to attack a note on the fourth string, the pick is positioned above the fourth string.

The pick makes contact with the third string at about a 45° angle.

The pick has attacked the third string and is resting on the second string.

The pick comes back through the third string at the same angle.

The pick is ready for the next attack somewhere above the fourth string.

As you become familiar with the pick attack motion, take notice of the wrist movement. It is possible you've already been playing this way since it is a natural motion. If so, great! If not, practice the steps slowly. Trying to go fast now will be a *big* waste of time.

The exercises

After becoming comfortable with the new pick attack, try playing the following examples. You'll notice the picking takes place on one string.

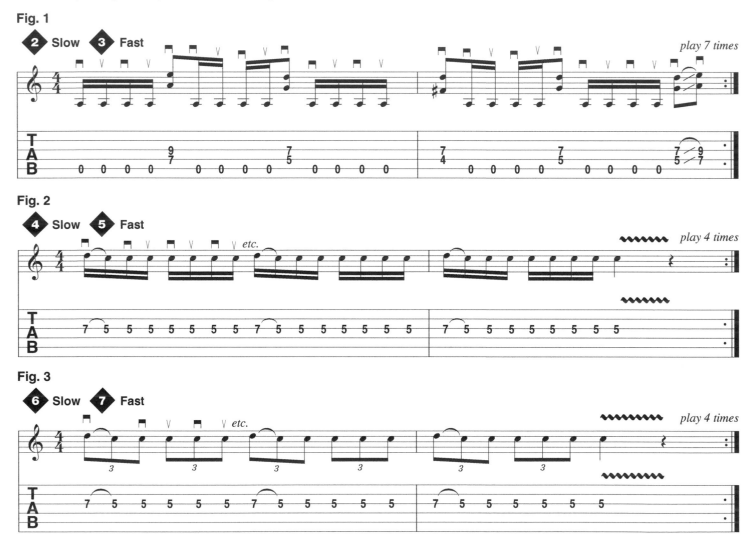

A *word about muting*: It's easier to learn how to mute at this point rather than later. Mute everything except chords. When you don't want muted notes move your hand back until it doesn't touch the strings.

A *word about picks*: Heavier gauge picks will give you a more confident attack. However, use whatever makes you feel comfortable. As for size, make sure you use a pick that feels good for both rhythm and lead. Both Danny and Nick use a typical "Fender-size" pick.

Hand synchronization

So far the exercises have been designed to familiarize you with using your wrist for picking. If you're feeling comfortable with the wrist, you're now ready to try something harder; synchronizing both hands.

The following exercises deal with one string at a time. This is so you don't waste any concentration on changing from one string to another. For now, concentrate on playing each note clearly. Move these exercises around—play them at different points on the fingerboard. Try them on all six strings. As always, use a metronome or a drum machine. Start very slowly and gradually increase your speed.

Fig. 4

Fig. 5

Because this next idea is from a pentatonic scale, it uses two strings.

Fig. 6

Here's a little ditty you can finish off your synchronization with.

Fig. 7

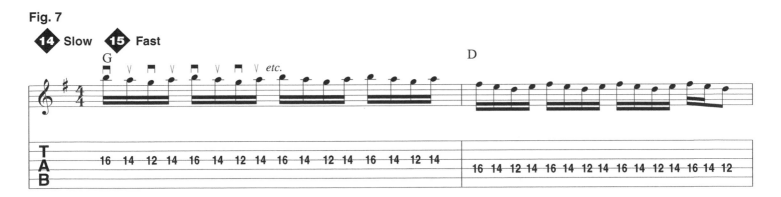

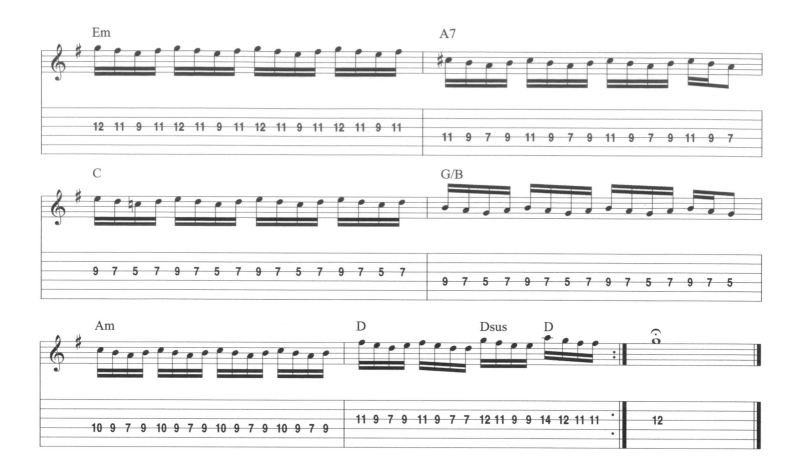

Changing strings

Now that you've mastered your wrist and synchronization, the next step is changing strings. Build on what you've learned. Your hand should look and feel the same on these next exercises as it did on Fig. 1. Sit in front of a mirror and play Fig. 1 up to speed. Check your picking hand. Now try Fig. 8. Does your hand look the same? If not, keep practicing until it does.

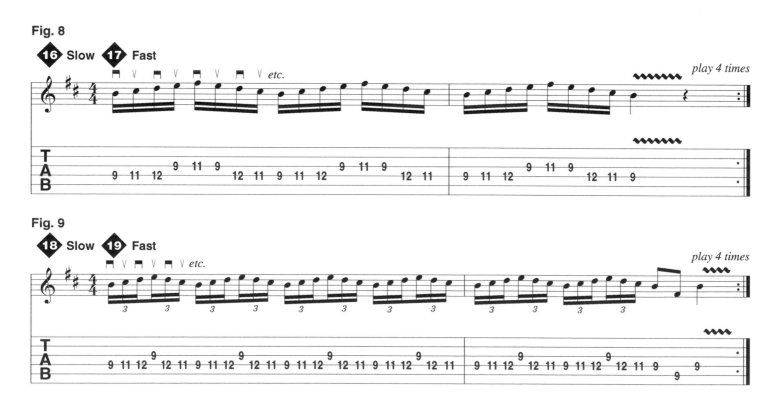

Fig. 10

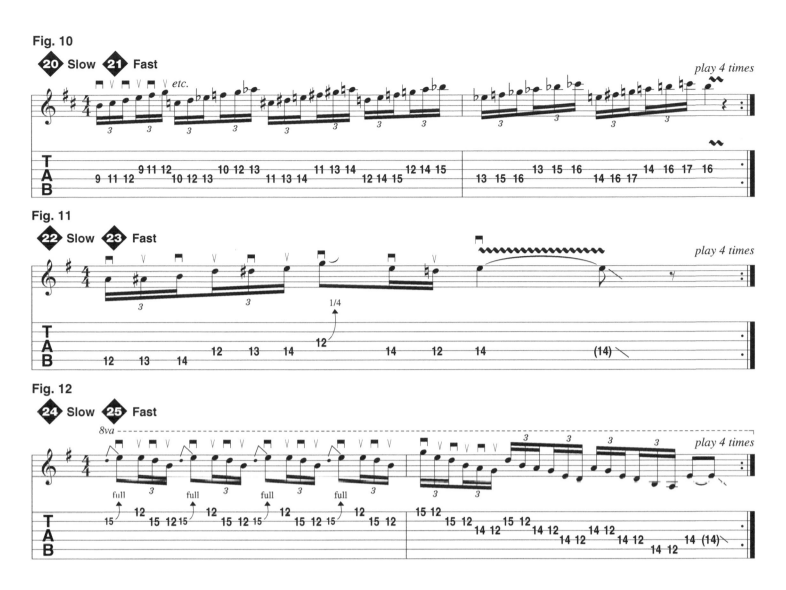

Fig. 11

Fig. 12

Application

Hopefully you've had a couple months of practice since you started this picking stuff. If not, you are a bit more advanced or you skimmed over the other sections too quickly. If you fall into the second category, make sure you've nailed every section.

Here's where it all comes together and stops sounding like exercises. The following licks are designed to get the new picking technique into your everyday playing. Pay attention to the key and remember what you've learned in the previous sections.

Fig. 13

Fig. 14

Fig. 15

Fig. 16

Now let's try examples 13–16 straight through as a solo.

30 **Figures 13–16 as a solo**

CHAPTER 2
THREE-NOTE-PER-STRING SCALES

In our first book, *Rock Lead Basics*, we presented five patterns of both diatonic and pentatonic scales. In this chapter we're going to expose you to *three-note-per-string scales*. These patterns should help fill in any "gray" areas you may still have. While these shapes are most commonly associated with the diatonic scale, any scale can be played as a three-note-per-string scale. For the purposes of this book, we're going to focus mainly on the diatonic scale. Once you feel comfortable with these seven shapes, take a look at the three-note-per-string shapes for the pentatonic and blues scales.

Since there are seven notes in the diatonic scale, there will be seven three-note-per-string patterns—one starting on each note of the scale. The major roots have been circled. These patterns are named in a way you may find confusing if you haven't read *Rock Lead Basics*. In that book, you learned the five diatonic scale patterns with the G.I.T. numbering system. Rather than naming the three-note-per-string patterns 1 through 7 (which would seem easiest), we've named them to match the five patterns presented in *Rock Lead Basics* and all other M.I. Press books.

Fig. 17: Three-note-per-string scales

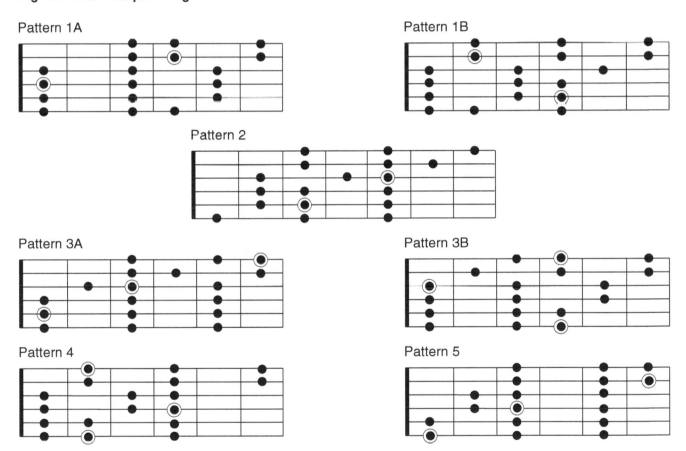

These next five patterns of the minor pentatonic scale use repeated notes so they are easier to play in one position. There is still a lot of stretching. These are all in E minor pentatonic.

Fig. 18: E minor pentatonic three-note-per-string scales

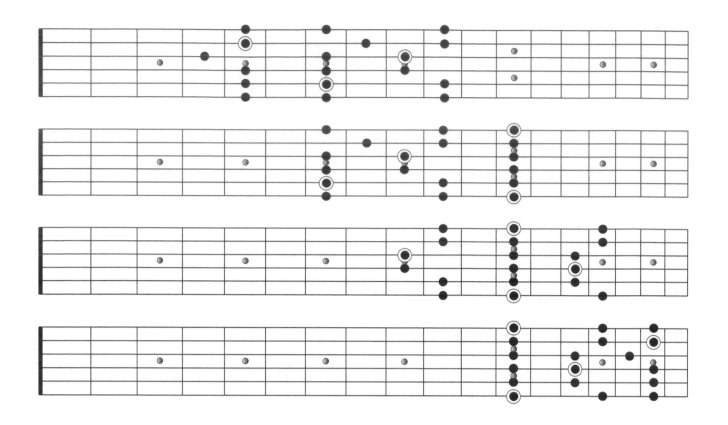

Here's something a little different—the blues scale on three notes per string. These are the two most useful patterns for this scale. The key is "A blues" (A minor pentatonic with the ♭5).

Fig. 19: Three-note-per-string A blues scale

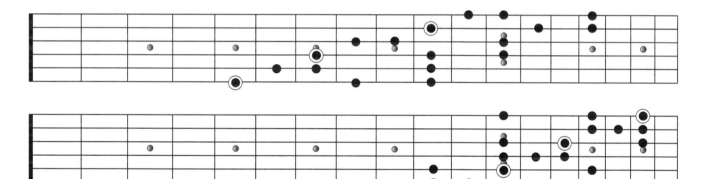

CHAPTER 3
PICKING LICKS

Sequences

Did you ever hear someone play a really cool scale run and land on just the right note? Chances are it wasn't luck; it was probably a sequence someone had practiced over and over again so they knew exactly what they were doing. What is a *sequence?* A sequence is an arrangement of notes with a repetitive pattern. The order of these notes is almost unlimited. We'll give you a few of our favorites, but feel free to make up your own.

Look below at Fig. 20. This is a popular sequence called "groups of four." It goes through the scale notes like this: 1–2–3–4, 2–3–4–5, 3–4–5–6, etc. Here it is in G Major, using pattern 5:

31 **Fig. 20: Groups of Four sequence**

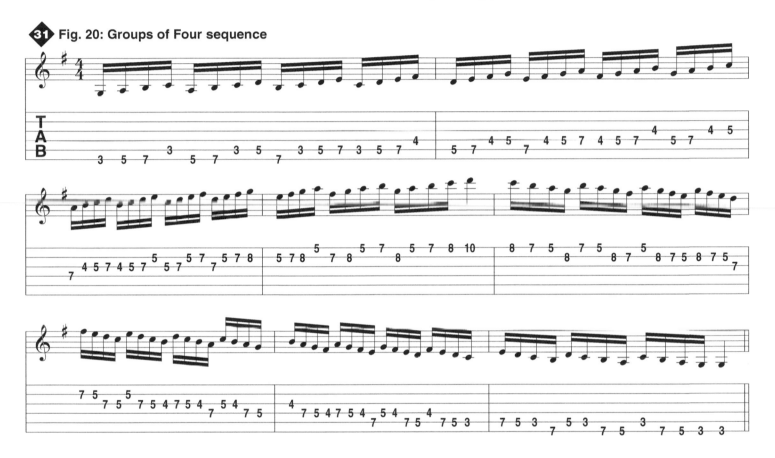

When working on the above sequence you'll notice something that is a bit difficult: the eighth and ninth notes in measure 3—these notes are both on the fifth fret, on *different* strings (this also happens with the twelfth and thirteenth notes in the same measure). This is a tough situation. Some people try to fret both notes at the same time, but the sequence ends up sounding sloppy because both notes ring out. Other people fret one note, then lift their finger off and *jump* to the next note. This is too slow. Try rolling your finger (in this case your index finger) from one note to the next. Follow the series of pictures below:

Fret the note C (eighth fret of the first string) with your third finger semi-flat— then attack the note.

Roll your finger towards the second string (without letting any pressure off the fingerboard).

The following is a rolling lick. Be sure to follow the steps from the previous page. The goal is to not jump between notes or have two notes ringing at the same time.

Fig. 21

Here's a lick that uses some tough sequencing… good luck!

Fig. 22

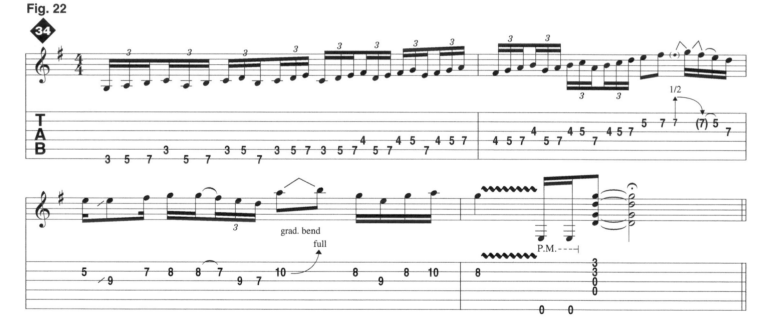

Let's try a Pentatonic sequence. Here's the A Minor Pentatonic Scale:

Fig. 23: A minor pentatonic minor scale

In this first example I'm going to ascend the scale in thirds. If you understand this concept on paper it will be a lot easier on the guitar. Follow along closely. The notes of the A minor pentatonic scale are as follows:

A–C–D–E–G–(A)

If we ascend in thirds (every other note), we get the following sequence:

A–D, C–E, D–G, E–A

To descend, simply reverse the notes. Figure 24 shows this sequence ascending and descending. Give the tracks a listen and try this out for yourself.

Fig. 24

This sequence starts on the third note of A minor pentatonic (D) and then plays back down the scale to the first note (A). Continue this group-of-three sequence until you reach the top of the A minor pentatonic scale. Figure 25 shows this sequence, along with a good way to come back down. Take a listen to the tracks and try it yourself.

Fig. 25

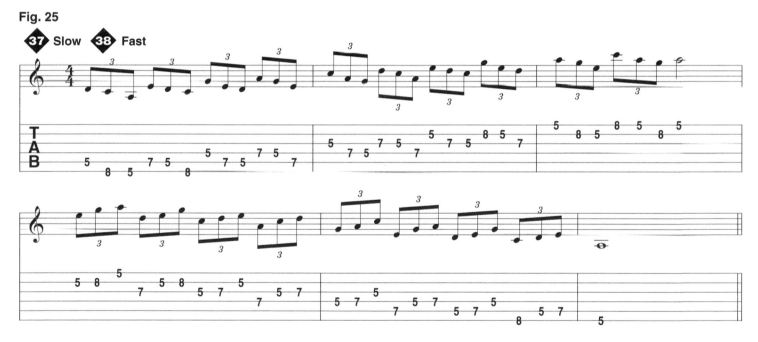

As you learn these new sequences, its a good idea to try and throw little bits of them into your playing. Notice how figure 26 uses this group-of-three pattern over a riff in A.

Fig. 26

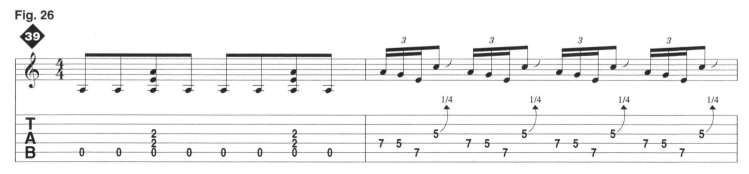

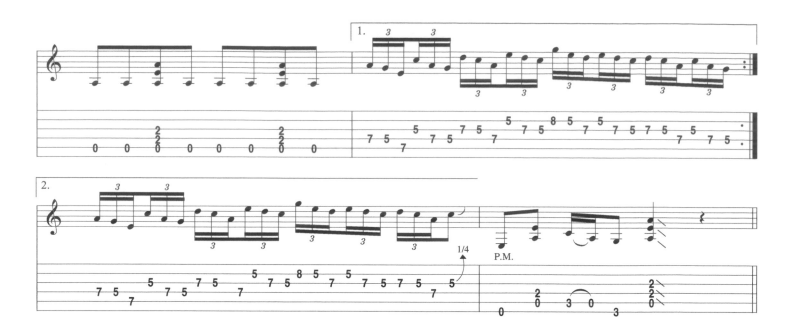

Now let's try a lick using a group-of-four sequence with the A blues scale. Remember: the A blues scale is the same as the minor pentatonic scale with the addition of the ♭5.

Fig. 27: A blues scale

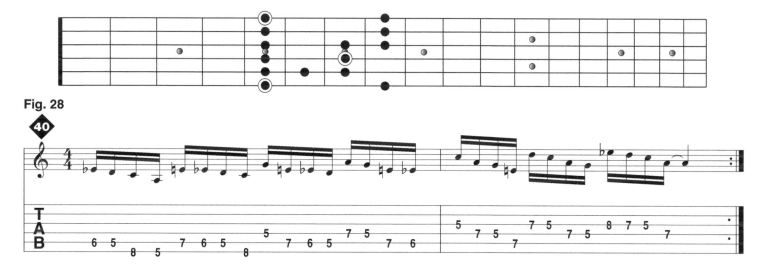

Fig. 28

Here's something a little different: the pentatonic scale in a group of five. Even though this sequence is a group of five, the phrasing is in sixteenth notes. Here's the pattern both ascending and descending.

Fig. 29

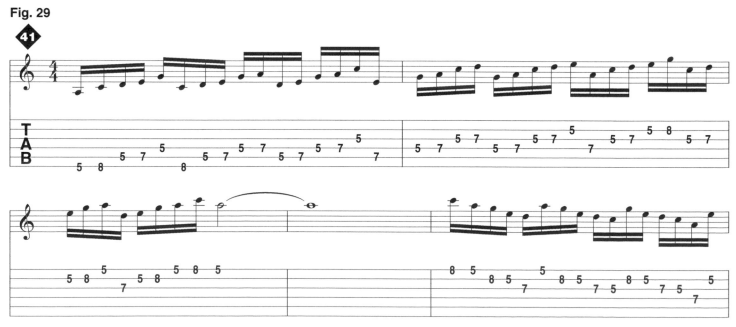

Now let's get back to the diatonic scale. These next two examples take advantage of the three-note-per-string scales presented in Chapter 2. Figure 30 is an eight-note sequence in G major requiring two strings to complete each sequence. It's a lot easier when broken down into pairs of strings. All six strings at once can be overwhelming.

Fig. 30

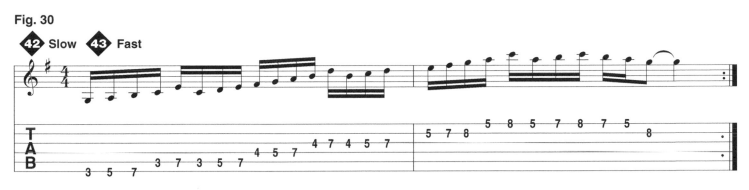

Here's a descending pattern using the same G major scale.

Fig. 31

Licks

If we shorten up a sequence and repeat a few notes we get some *licks*. Here are a few of my favorites.

The first one combines descending fifths and fourths in E minor. Watch out for those first finger slides!

Fig. 32

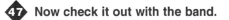 Now check it out with the band.

The blue note (♭5) can be a great addition to your licks—both diatonic and pentatonic. These next two licks are from the G blues scale.

Fig. 33

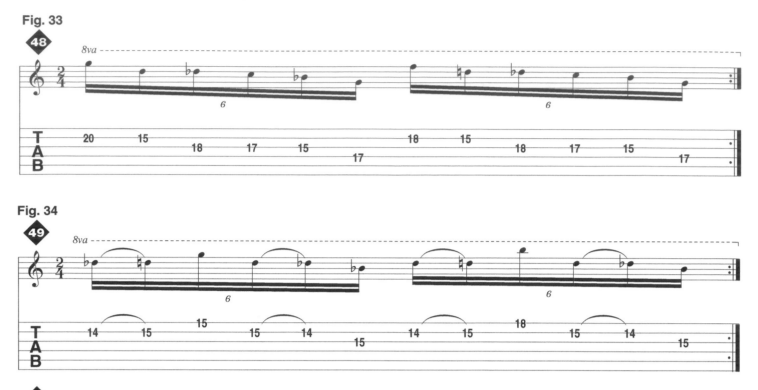

Fig. 34

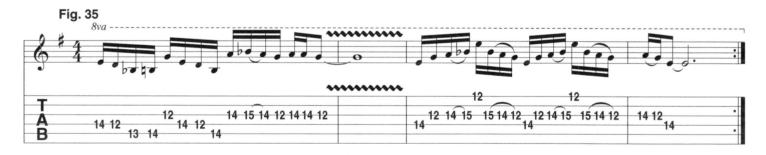

🔷50 Figs. 33 and 34 with band

String Skipping

String skipping is one of the hardest picking techniques. Not only do you have to jump the extra distance between the strings—you also have to figure out how to keep the unwanted strings quiet while you jump across them. However, if you can pull off a great string-skipping lick at the right time and place, you will not only be rewarded with the undying adulation of your peers—Publishers Clearing House may arrive at your door step with that oversized check for $1,000,000! Well, maybe not, but you can still try out some of these licks. As always, start slowly and play cleanly and evenly.

We'll start off with an easy one using the E blues scale:

Fig. 35

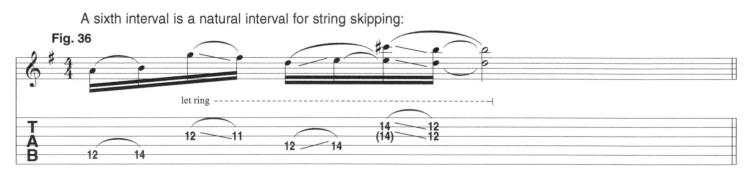

A sixth interval is a natural interval for string skipping:

Fig. 36

🔷51 Fig. 36 and 35 with band

18

Here's a longer idea in E major.

Fig. 37

Now here's something similar in C# minor—the relative minor scale of E major.

Fig. 38

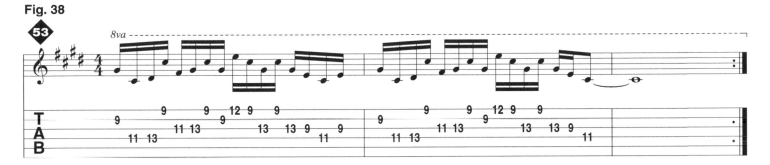

For our final workout lets combine some of these shapes. If you can pull this off your technique is happening!

Fig. 39

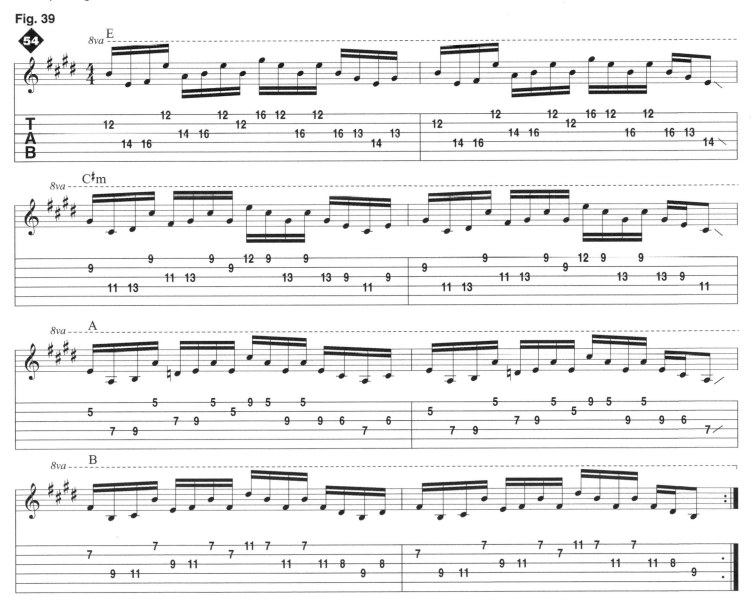

Fingerpicking *(using the fingers of the picking hand to attack notes)*

Fingerpicking or "Chicken Pickin'" is a technique that has crossed over from country guitar to rock. It can add a lot to your playing and make many licks easier to play. If you still don't know what "Chicken Pickin'" sounds like, listen to Tracks 63–64.

The concept is simple. Watch the series of pictures below.

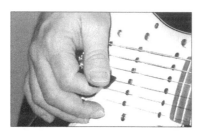

Use your pick as you normally would.

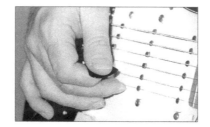

Rest your middle finger on the string.

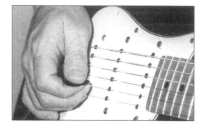

Pluck your finger upward. It's o.k. to snap the string. In fact, it sounds cool.

Let's get started with an easy one. Try the figure below. The notes with the "m" over them are meant to be plucked with your middle finger. The "m" comes from classical guitar notation:

p (pulgar) = thumb

i (indice) = index finger

m (medio) = middle finger

a (anular) = ring finger

Fig. 40

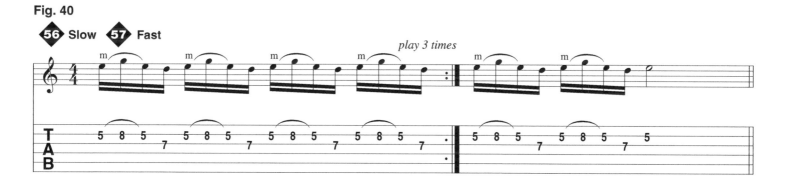

Here's another; this one is a bit more demanding.

Fig. 41

Try the following diatonic three-note-per-string idea.

Fig. 42

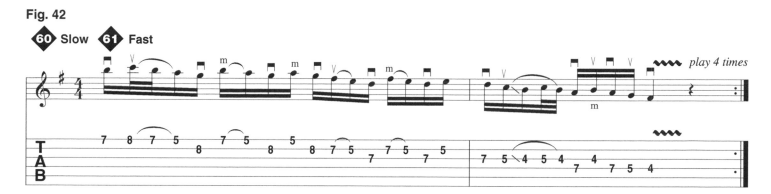

Here's an interesting sound. Have you ever heard of inverted thirds (sixths)? Look at the figure below. This is the E Mixolydian scale in inverted thirds (There'll be more about the Mixolydian scale in the next book. As for now, realize that this scale works for an E blues song). Play this scale with the pick on the third string and your middle finger plucking the first string.

Fig. 43

*Key signature denotes E Mixolydian

Now we'll take that same scale and put some funk in it.

Fig. 44

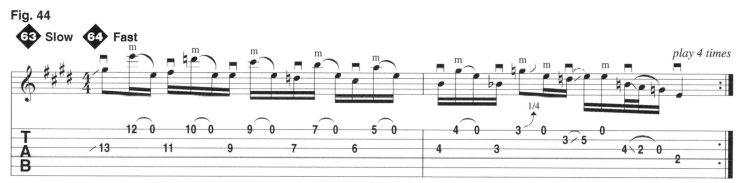

Finally, here's a way to travel the whole neck using fingerpicking.

Fig. 45

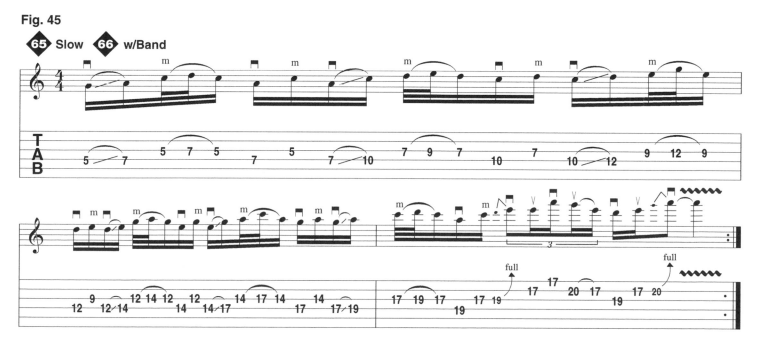

CHAPTER 4
SWEEP PICKING

Simply stated, *sweep picking* is the technique where your pick moves in one direction across a set of strings; it is the opposite technique of alternate picking. Sounds easy right? It can be, but the hard part is making each individual note stand out on its own. If the notes ring together, your "sweeps" will simply sound like chords!

Let's get right into it. Start slowly and play cleanly.

Fig. 46

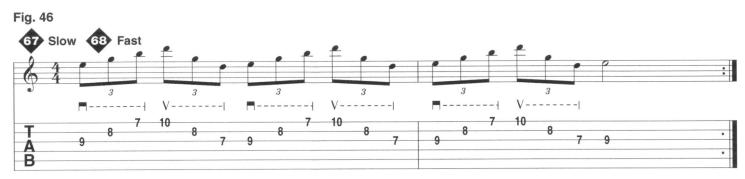

If you're having trouble with this, try following these simple steps:

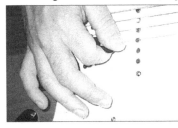

With your picking hand, strike the
first note on the G string.
As you ascend the first lick,
pick downwards (towards the floor).

Without lifting up your pick, glide across
the G string to the B string.

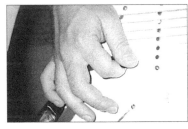

Continue this through to the
high E string.

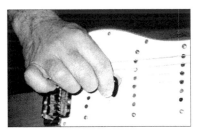

To reverse this lick, pick upwards
towards the ceiling, gliding smoothly
across each string. Try not to lift up with
your pick as you switch strings.

If you still sound sloppy, try *muting* heavily with the side of your picking hand. The easiest way to do this is to rest your picking hand at or near the bridge of the guitar. This will help anchor your picking hand and give you greater stability. (see picture below)

As a general rule when sweep picking, it is a good idea to use hammer-ons and pull-offs when you have more than one note on a given string. Check out Fig. 47 for this idea.

Fig. 47

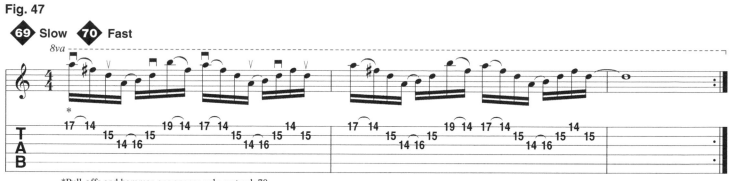

*Pull-offs and hammer-ons appear only on track 70.

Now let's add a *slide* to a sweep lick. This lick will outline two major triad *arpeggios*—E major and D major (an arpeggio is defined as "the notes of a chord in scale form").

Fig. 48

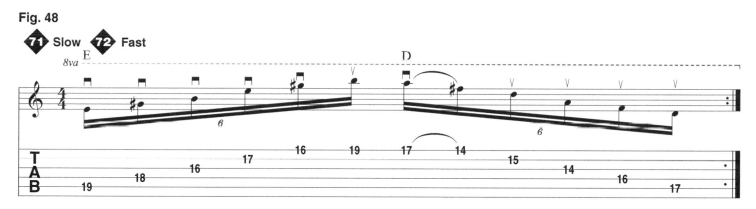

Sweep picking is commonly associated with arpeggios because arpeggios often contain only one note per string. Here's a few of my favorites. I've included the fingerings because they have worked well for me, but they are only suggestions. The rule of thumb is "if it feels good, it is good!"

Fig. 49: E Minor Arpeggio

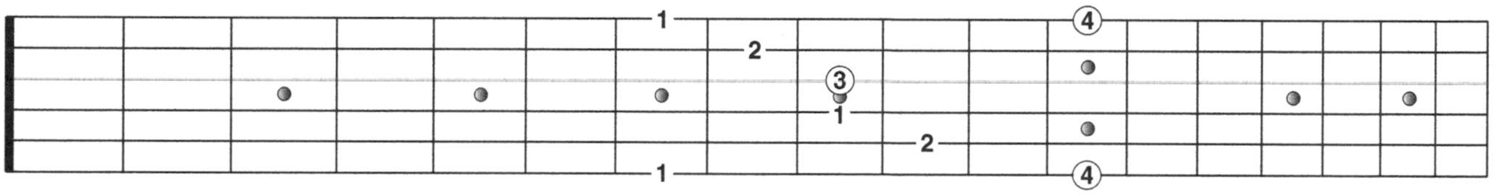

Fig. 50: E Minor 11 Arpeggio

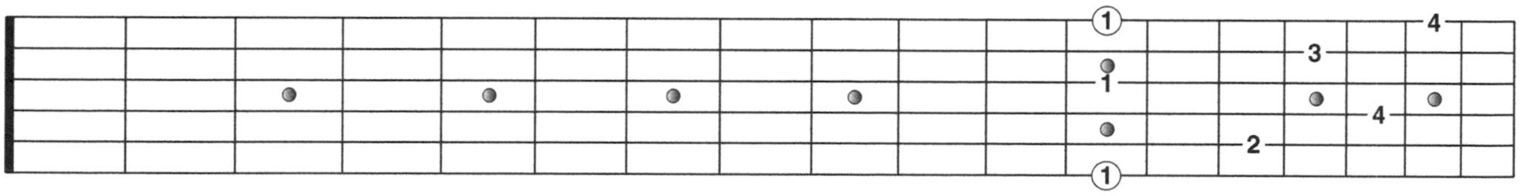

Fig. 51: D$_9^6$ Arpeggio

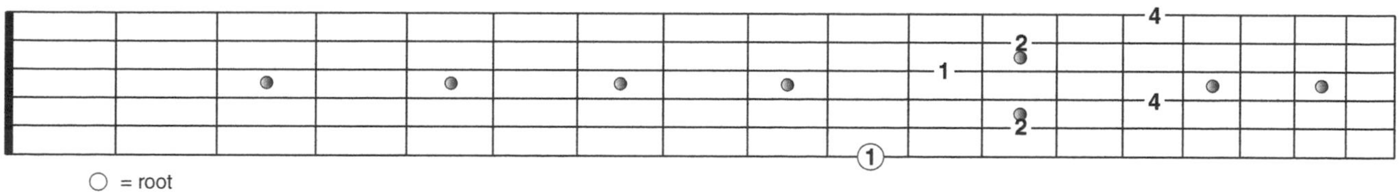

○ = root

Now let's apply some of these ideas over a chord progression. The key center will be E minor:

Fig. 52

Your turn. Feel free to use any of the licks or arpeggios from this chapter—or better yet, make up your own!

Fig. 53

Here are a few more arpeggios—the dominant 7 and the major 7. The sound will be quite different than what we've played so far, but the sweep picking technique is the same.

Fig. 54: E7 Arpeggio

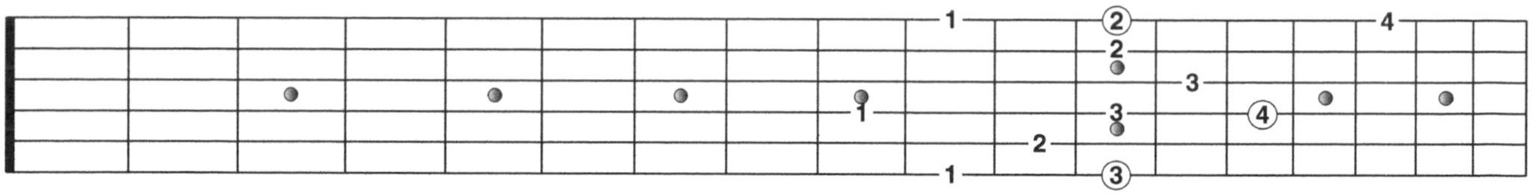

Fig. 55: E Major 7 Arpeggio

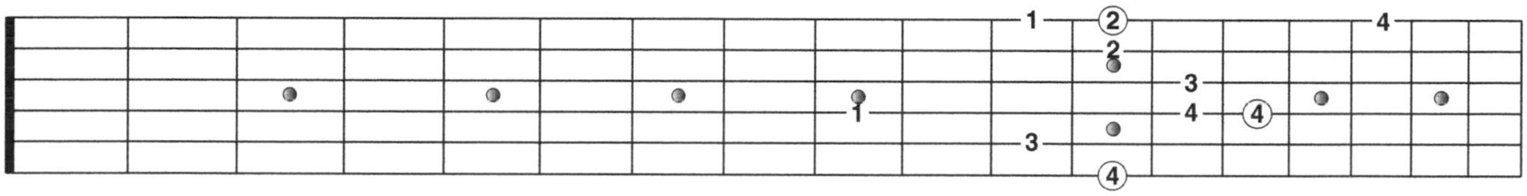

Fig. 56: A Major Arpeggio

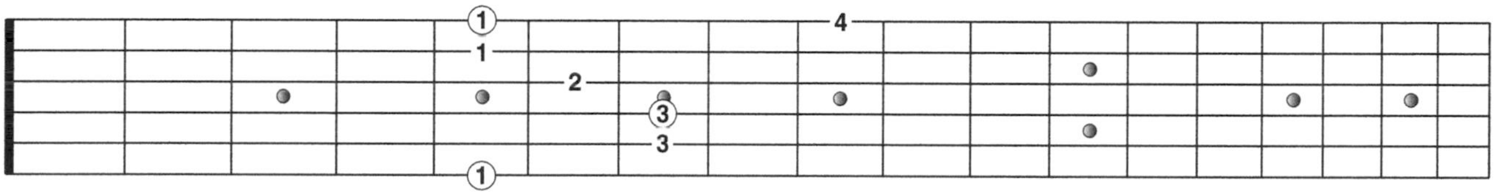

Fig. 57: E Major Arpeggio

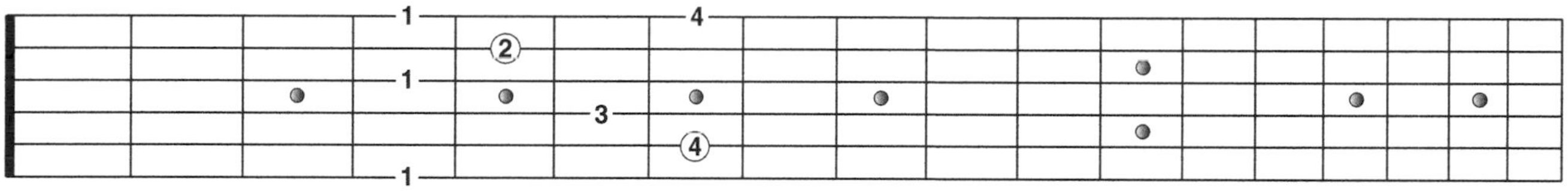

○ = root

Here's an exercise using major arpeggios on all six strings. This one has a classical flavor to it.

Fig. 58

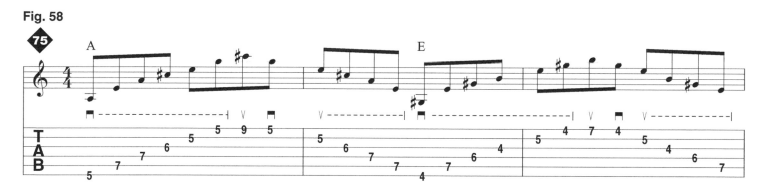

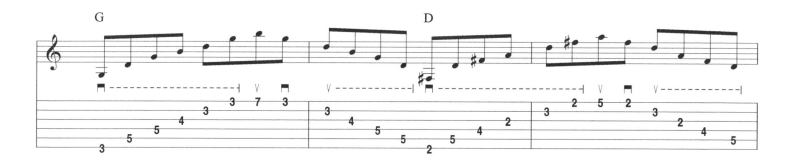

For our last example we're going to get a little heavier. Check out how these sweeps outline the chords in this progression.

Fig. 59

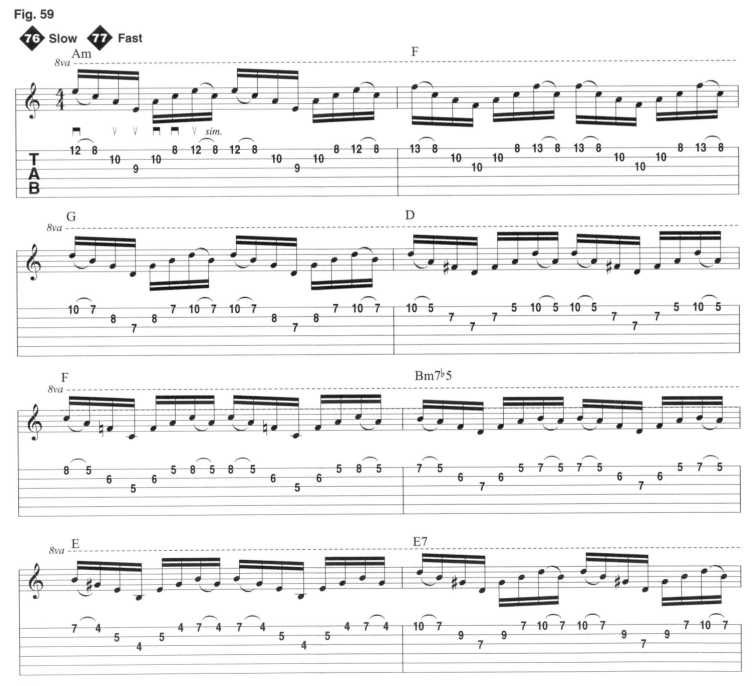

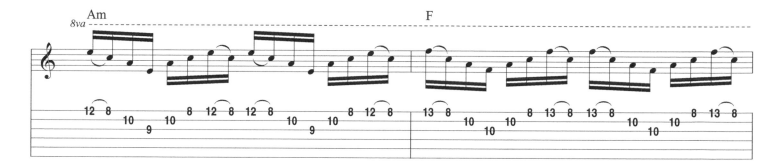

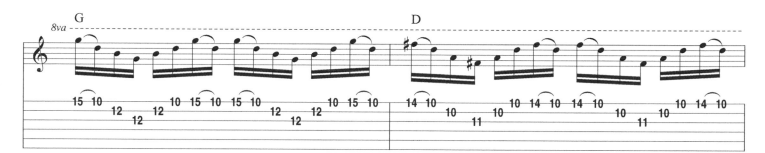

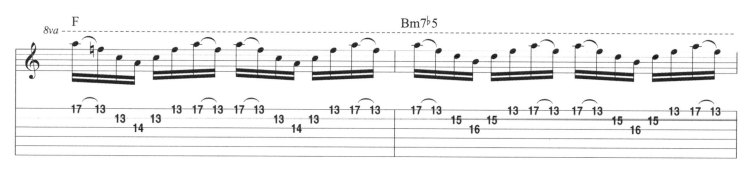

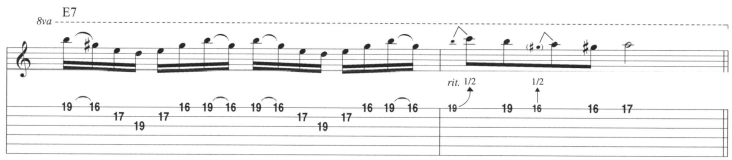

Keep in mind that there is no "right" way to pick. You'll probably use many different techniques—maybe even in the same solo. The goal is to have control so you can play what you feel. If you can do that, you've accomplished something!

Finally, a track to jam along with. Have some fun!

Fig. 60

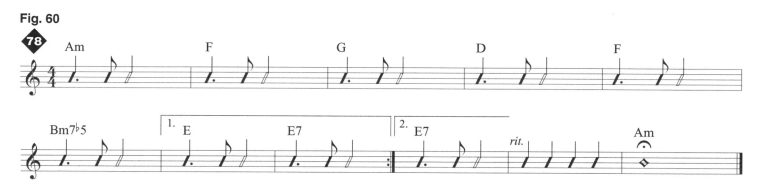

CHAPTER 5
HARMONICS

Harmonics can add a whole new and exciting dimension to your playing. With the use of harmonics you can create a variety of sounds from shimmering, clean rhythm patterns to screaming, over-the-top lead lines and anything in between.

What exactly is a *harmonic?* The dictionary defines a harmonic as "a tone produced on a stringed instrument by lightly touching an open or stopped (fretted) note at a given fraction of its length so both segments vibrate."

Fancy definitions aside, you should know in order to play harmonics effectively *you must play on top of the fret wire*—not in between the frets.

In this chapter we're going to take a look at three types of harmonics: natural harmonics, fretted harmonics, and pinch harmonics.

Natural harmonics

Natural Harmonics are harmonics that occur on each open string of the guitar. The strongest of these open-string harmonics seems to be on the twelfth fret. This is because the twelfth fret on the guitar is exactly half the distance between the nut and the bridge of the guitar.

Start by placing your fretting hand on top of the twelfth fret.

Now pick the strings as you normally would. If you do this correctly you should be able to leave your finger on the string and still hear the harmonic ring (but most commonly you should lift your finger immediately after striking the note). Practice this first step slowly until the notes are clear and have lots of sustain. Next move on to the seventh fret and then to the fifth fret.

Fig. 61

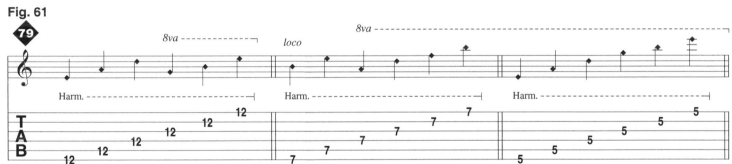

Now let's apply some of these harmonics over a simple chord progression in E minor.

Fig. 62

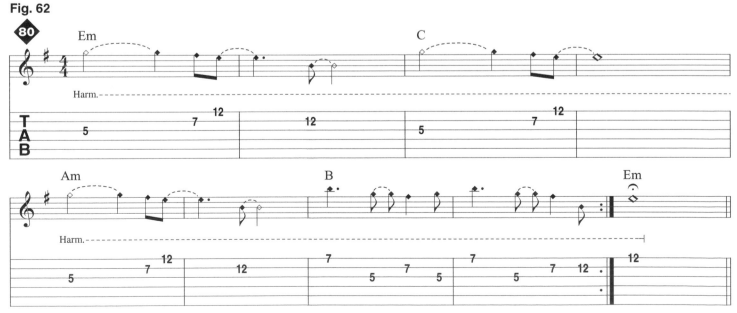

28

The pitch of the harmonic at the twelfth fret is the same as the name of the open string. In other words, if you play a harmonic on the twelfth fret of the D string, the pitch will also be D. However, some frets will produce notes other than the name of the open string which you are playing. Take a look at Fig. 63 for a brief rundown of open-string natural harmonics.

Fig. 63

Notice these natural harmonics outline a major triad of the string you're on. In other words, the harmonics on the A string outline the notes of an A major chord (A is the root; C♯ is the major third; and E is the fifth). In this next example we're going to take advantage of these harmonics to create a more "major" sound. Remember, the fourth fret harmonic is a major third of the string you're on (see Fig. 63).

Fig. 64

Here's some harmonics combined with a simple I–IV–V chord progression in E. Check out how the harmonics fit over each chord.

Fig. 65: Blues in E with Harmonics

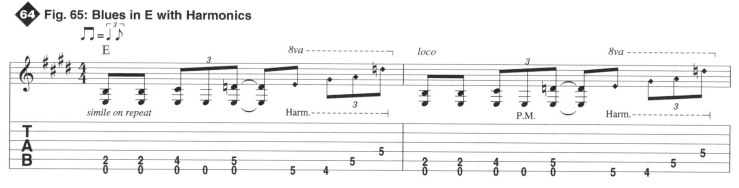

While these are the most common open-string harmonics, some others are possible. Figures 66 and 67 show where to get a 9th and a ♭7. These may be tough, but they're there.

Fig. 66: the 9th

Fig. 67: the ♭7

*Note: Figure 67—the ♭7 harmonic—is an exception to the "on top of the fret" rule. For this harmonic, place your finger on top of the string in between the second and third fret.

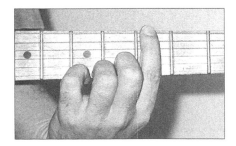

Fretted harmonics

Fretted harmonics allow you to play any note as a harmonic—not just the open string notes. The harmonics from a fretted note will occur at the same intervals as that of the open string harmonics. For instance, if you play the note E on the second fret of the D string, you can create the harmonic of the note E one octave (twelve frets) above the second fret. This means one of the possible harmonic overtones of the second fret E will occur at the fourteenth fret.

The question is—how do you get the harmonic to ring? There are two common ways:

Tap harmonics

This is when you "tap" or "pop" the string with your picking hand at a specific interval above the fretted note. Remember: you must tap *on top of* the fret wire. Most people use their first finger, but any finger will do.

Listen to the next track. First I'll play the note E on the second fret of the D string. Next I'll tap the harmonic above the fourteenth fret. Listen to the results and then try it out for yourself.

Fig. 68

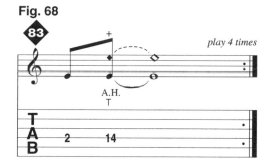

The following figure gives you an idea of which harmonics are possible from a fretted E note at the second fret of the D string.

Fig. 69

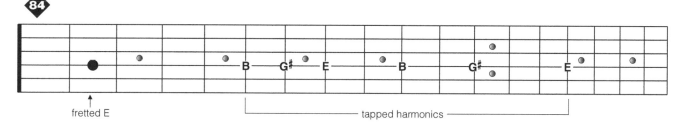

Listen and then try these tapped harmonics out for yourself. It may take some time to get the hang of this technique—after all, it is pretty hard. Try not to get too frustrated.

Our next track combines open string harmonics with tapping harmonics.

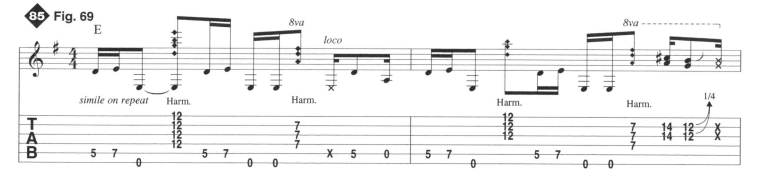

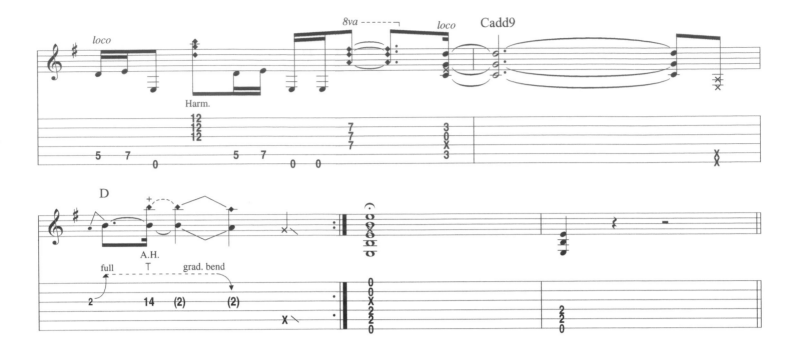

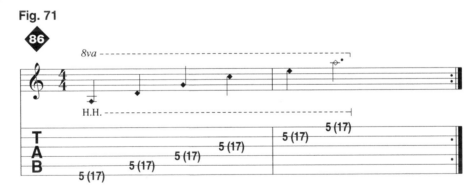

Harp Harmonics

Along with tapping, another common method of fretting harmonics is known as *harp harmonics*. For this technique follow these simple steps:

   A. Place your first finger on the harmonic to be plucked. (see picture)

   B. Place your thumb behind your first finger on the same string. (see picture)

   C. Using your thumb as a pick, "pluck" the harmonic with your picking hand.

Let's try this with a clean tone. While barring fret 5, pluck the harmonics on the seventeenth fret.

Fig. 71

Let's go ahead and try this technique out with the band. This next phrase uses the A blues scale. On the track I'll play the riff first without harmonics and then with the harp harmonics. Check out the difference.

Fig. 72

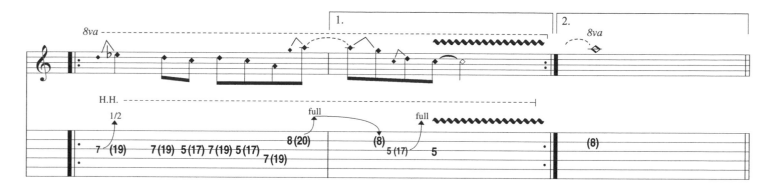

When used in combination with notes that are not harmonics, this harp technique can create some awesome chord patterns. Follow these steps slowly.

Barre the fifth fret.

With the third finger of your picking hand, pick the D string—not the harmonic.

With your first finger creating the harmonic of the seventeenth fret, use your thumbnail to pluck the low E string.

The possible combinations of picked notes and harmonic notes are endless, but for now let's continue this way:

Fig. 73

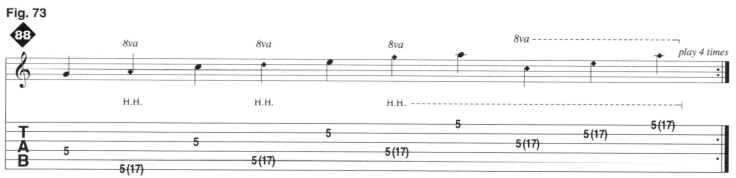

Pinch harmonics

The final type of harmonics we're going to talk about is *pinch harmonics*. These harmonics are created by "pinching" the strings with a combination of your pick and the side of your thumb (see picture at right).

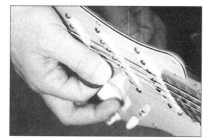

Pinch harmonics are different than the previous harmonics we've talked about because they can be created anywhere on the string. Lots of distortion can also be a big help.

Fig. 74

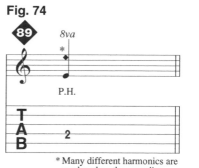

* Many different harmonics are produced on the recording, not just this one.

Start by "pinching" the note "E" on the second fret of the "D" string at or near the bridge and then move up the string slowly.

x

Now let's try a longer example.

Fig. 75

CHAPTER 6
SOLO CONSTRUCTION

How to create a solo for a song is a vast subject that could fill many books. There's no real method for making the perfect solo since every song is different. In this chapter we'll discuss some of the aspects that make a good solo.

Motifs and Answers

The word *motif* means: A short arrangement of notes that sounds "memorable." Think of Beethoven's Fifth Symphony: Da-Da-Da-DAAAAH. This is a good example of a motif.

As a rock guitarist, you should get used to making short phrases that sound memorable or even unusual. By playing this way, the audience will remember what you've played and it won't sound like just notes or scales. Once you've played your motif, back it up by playing it again, or play it just a bit differently. This will help make your idea last in the listener's ear. Try the figure below and notice its form. The first half has a shape to it that acts as a motif. The second two measures "answer" the first.

Fig. 76

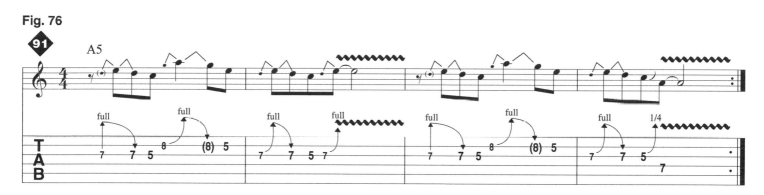

The figure below is another example of a motif and its answer. This time the motif gets its strength from the rhythmic figure combined with the interval skips. This doesn't sound like running a scale—it sounds like a musical statement.

Fig. 77

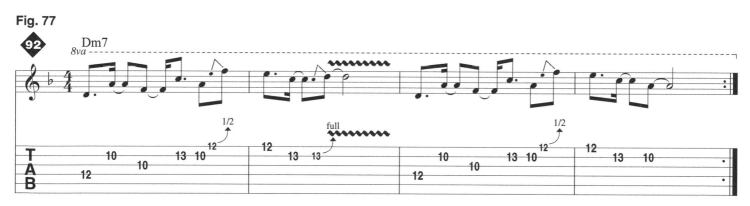

Development and climax

Now that you have some experience with motifs and their answers, the next step is to add development to a solo. This means expanding past your original statements. This would be a good place to use some of the material you learned earlier in the book. The idea here is to create a motif, answer that motif, then expand with maybe a scale sequence or two-handed lick (or whatever you think sounds good). After a bit of development, it's a good idea to go back to a motif. Finally, when the end of the solo is near, it's always a good idea to build the intensity to a climactic end. Learn the following figure and play along with the track.

Fig. 78

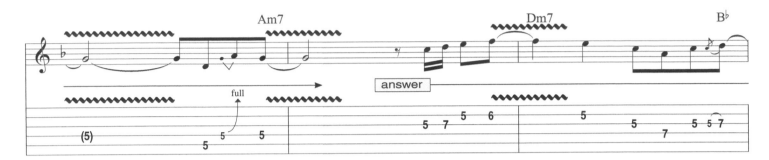

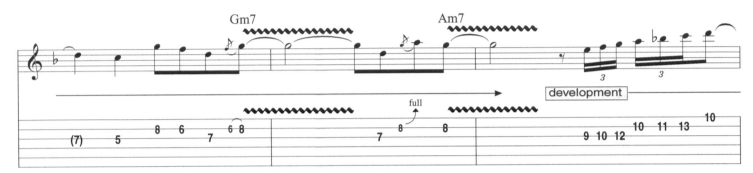

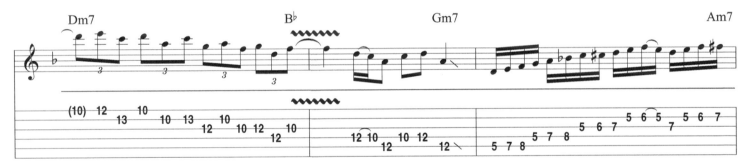

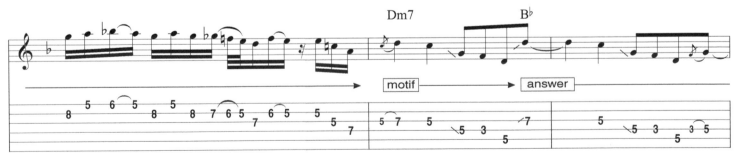

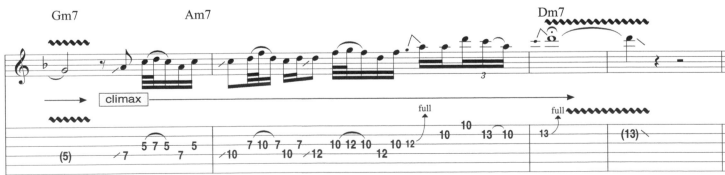

Balance

Regardless of the style of music, a soloist always needs a good sense of balance. I'm referring to the balance between high and low notes, fast and slow notes, double stops and single notes, and resting and playing. Simply being aware of this should make you a better player. If you play all high notes it can become boring for a listener. If you play fast all the time without stopping, it can sound too confusing. Listen to the rhythm track to the progression below. Try to get as much variety as possible in your solo. Then learn the solo to get some extra ideas.

Fig. 79

Fig. 80

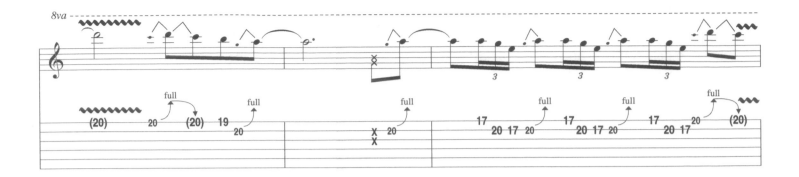

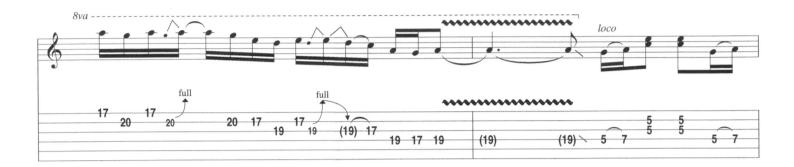

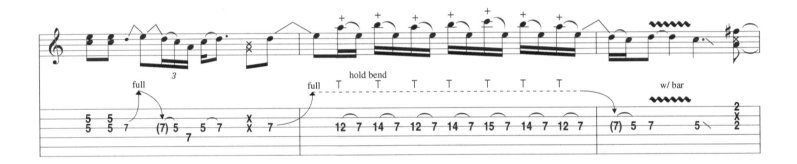

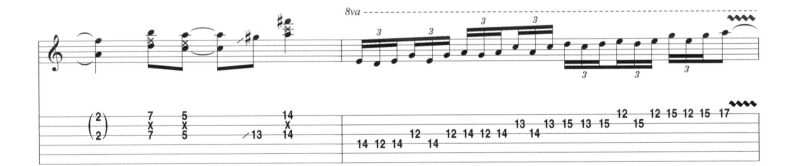

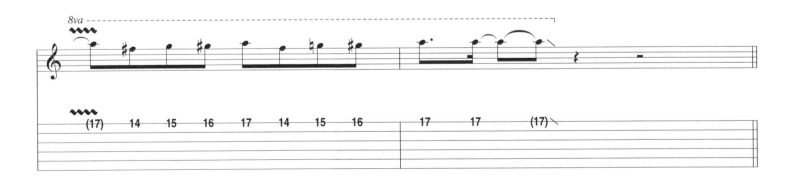

GUITAR NOTATION LEGEND

Guitar Music can be notated three different ways: on a *musical staff*, in *tablature*, and in *rhythm slashes*.

RHYTHM SLASHES are written above the staff. Strum chords in the rhythm indicated. Use the chord diagrams found at the top of the first page of the transcription for the appropriate chord voicings. Round noteheads indicate single notes.

THE MUSICAL STAFF shows pitches and rhythms and is divided by bar lines into measures. Pitches are named after the first seven letters of the alphabet.

TABLATURE graphically represents the guitar fingerboard. Each horizontal line represents a string, and each number represents a fret.

Notes:

Strings:

4th string, 2nd fret   1st & 2nd strings open,   open D chord
played together

HALF-STEP BEND: Strike the note and bend up 1/2 step.

WHOLE-STEP BEND: Strike the note and bend up one step.

GRACE NOTE BEND: Strike the note and bend up as indicated. The first note does not take up any time.

SLIGHT (MICROTONE) BEND: Strike the note and bend up 1/4 step.

BEND AND RELEASE: Strike the note and bend up as indicated, then release back to the original note. Only the first note is struck.

PRE-BEND: Bend the note as indicated, then strike it.

VIBRATO: The string is vibrated by rapidly bending and releasing the note with the fretting hand.

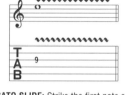

WIDE VIBRATO: The pitch is varied to a greater degree by vibrating with the fretting hand.

HAMMER-ON: Strike the first (lower) note with one finger, then sound the higher note (on the same string) with another finger by fretting it without picking.

PULL-OFF: Place both fingers on the notes to be sounded. Strike the first note and without picking, pull the finger off to sound the second (lower) note.

LEGATO SLIDE: Strike the first note and then slide the same fret-hand finger up or down to the second note. The second note is not struck.

SHIFT SLIDE: Same as legato slide, except the second note is struck.

TRILL: Very rapidly alternate between the notes indicated by continuously hammering on and pulling off.

TAPPING: Hammer ("tap") the fret indicated with the pick-hand index or middle finger and pull off to the note fretted by the fret hand.

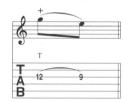

NATURAL HARMONIC: Strike the note while the fret-hand lightly touches the string directly over the fret indicated.

PINCH HARMONIC: The note is fretted normally and a harmonic is produced by adding the edge of the thumb or the tip of the index finger of the pick hand to the normal pick attack.

PICK SCRAPE: The edge of the pick is rubbed down (or up) the string, producing a scratchy sound.

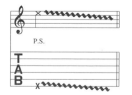

MUFFLED STRINGS: A percussive sound is produced by laying the fret hand across the string(s) without depressing, and striking them with the pick hand.

PALM MUTING: The note is partially muted by the pick hand lightly touching the string(s) just before the bridge.

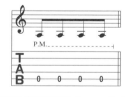

RAKE: Drag the pick across the strings indicated with a single motion.

TREMOLO PICKING: The note is picked as rapidly and continuously as possible.

VIBRATO BAR DIVE AND RETURN: The pitch of the note or chord is dropped a specified number of steps (in rhythm) then returned to the original pitch.

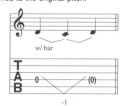

VIBRATO BAR SCOOP: Depress the bar just before striking the note, then quickly release the bar.

VIBRATO BAR DIP: Strike the note and then immediately drop a specified number of steps, then release back to the original pitch.

MUSICIANS INSTITUTE PRESS is the official series of Southern California's renowned music school, Musicians Institute. MI instructors, some of the finest musicians in the world, share their vast knowledge and experience with you – no matter what your current level. For guitar, bass, drums, vocals, and keyboards, MI Press offers the finest music curriculum for higher learning through a variety of series:

ESSENTIAL CONCEPTS
Designed from MI core curriculum programs.

MASTER CLASS
Designed from MI elective courses.

PRIVATE LESSONS
Tackle a variety of topics "one-on one" with MI faculty instructors.

GUITAR

Acoustic Artistry
by Evan Hirschelman • Private Lessons
00695922 Book/Online Audio $24.99

Advanced Scale Concepts & Licks for Guitar
by Jean Marc Belkadi • Private Lessons
00695298 Book/CD Pack $22.99

All-in-One Guitar Soloing Course
by Daniel Gilbert & Beth Marlis
00217709 Book/Online Media $29.99

Blues/Rock Soloing for Guitar
by Robert Calva • Private Lessons
00695680 Book/Online Audio $22.99

Blues Guitar Soloing
by Keith Wyatt • Master Class
00695132 Book/Online Audio $29.99

Blues Rhythm Guitar
by Keith Wyatt • Master Class
00695131 Book/Online Audio $22.99

Dean Brown
00696002 DVD $29.95

Chord Progressions for Guitar
by Tom Kolb • Private Lessons
00695664 Book/Online Audio $19.99

Chord Tone Soloing
by Barrett Tagliarino • Private Lessons
00695855 Book/Online Audio $27.99

Chord-Melody Guitar
by Bruce Buckingham • Private Lessons
00695646 Book/Online Audio $22.99

Classical & Fingerstyle Guitar Techniques
by David Oakes • Master Class
00695171 Book/Online Audio $22.99

Classical Themes for Electric Guitar
by Jean Marc Belkadi • Private Lessons
00695806 Book/CD Pack $15.99

Country Guitar
by Al Bonhomme • Master Class
00695661 Book/Online Audio $22.99

Essential Rhythm Guitar
by Steve Trovato • Private Lessons
00695181 Book/CD Pack $16.99

Exotic Scales & Licks for Electric Guitar
by Jean Marc Belkadi • Private Lessons
00695860 Book/CD Pack $19.99

Funk Guitar
by Ross Bolton • Private Lessons
00695419 Book/Online Audio $17.99

Guitar Basics
by Bruce Buckingham • Private Lessons
00695134 Book/Online Audio $19.99

Guitar Fretboard Workbook
by Barrett Tagliarino • Essential Concepts
00695712 . . . . $22.99

Guitar Hanon
by Peter Deneff • Private Lessons
00695321 . . . . $17.99

Guitar Lick•tionary
by Dave Hill • Private Lessons
00695482 Book/CD Pack $22.99

Guitar Soloing
by Dan Gilbert & Beth Marlis • Essential Concepts
00695190 Book/Online Audio $24.99

Harmonics
by Jamie Findlay • Private Lessons
00695169 Book/CD Pack $16.99

Harmony & Theory
by Keith Wyatt & Carl Schroeder • Essential Concepts
00695161 . . . . $24.99

Introduction to Jazz Guitar Soloing
by Joe Elliott • Master Class
00695406 Book/Online Audio $24.99

Jazz Guitar Chord System
by Scott Henderson • Private Lessons
00695291 . . . . $14.99

Jazz Guitar Improvisation
by Sid Jacobs • Master Class
00217711 Book/Online Media $19.99

Jazz, Rock & Funk Guitar
by Dean Brown • Private Lessons
00217690 Book/Online Media $19.99

Latin Guitar
by Bruce Buckingham • Master Class
00695379 Book/Online Audio $19.99

Lead Sheet Bible
by Robin Randall & Janice Peterson • Private Lessons
00695130 Book/Online Audio $24.99

Liquid Legato
by Allen Hinds • Private Lessons
00696656 Book/Online Audio $17.99

Modern Jazz Concepts for Guitar
by Sid Jacobs • Master Class
00695711 Book/CD Pack $19.99

Modern Rock Rhythm Guitar
by Danny Gill • Private Lessons
00695682 Book/Online Audio $22.99

Modes for Guitar
by Tom Kolb • Private Lessons
00695555 Book/Online Audio $19.99

Music Reading for Guitar
by David Oakes • Essential Concepts
00695192 . . . . $24.99

Outside Guitar Licks
by Jean Marc Belkadi • Private Lessons
00695697 Book/CD Pack $16.99

Power Plucking
by Dale Turner • Private Lesson
00695962 Book/CD Pack $19.95

Progressive Tapping Licks
by Jean Marc Belkadi • Private Lessons
00695748 Book/CD Pack $19.99

Rhythm Guitar
by Bruce Buckingham & Eric Paschal • Essential Concepts
00695188 Book $22.99
00114559 Book/Online Audio $27.99
00695909 DVD $19.95

Rhythmic Lead Guitar
by Barrett Tagliarino • Private Lessons
00110263 Book/Online Audio $22.99

Rock Lead Basics
by Nick Nolan & Danny Gill • Master Class
00695144 Book/Online Audio $19.99

Rock Lead Performance
by Nick Nolan & Danny Gill • Master Class
00695278 Book/Online Audio $19.99

Rock Lead Techniques
by Nick Nolan & Danny Gill • Master Class
00695146 Book/Online Audio $19.99

Shred Guitar
by Greg Harrison • Master Class
00695977 Book/Online Audio $24.99

Solo Slap Guitar
by Jude Gold • Master Class
00139556 Book/Online Video $24.99

Technique Exercises for Guitar
by Jean Marc Belkadi • Private Lessons
00695913 Book/CD Pack $17.99

Texas Blues Guitar
by Robert Calva • Private Lessons
00695340 Book/Online Audio $19.99

Ultimate Guitar Technique
by Bill LaFleur • Private Lessons
00695863 Book/Online Audio $24.99

Prices, contents, and availability subject to change without notice.

HAL•LEONARD®
7777 W. BLUEMOUND RD. P.O. BOX 13819 MILWAUKEE, WI 53213
www.halleonard.com